Original title:
The Front Door of Dreams

Copyright © 2025 Creative Arts Management OÜ
All rights reserved.

Author: Zachary Prescott
ISBN HARDBACK: 978-1-80587-185-9
ISBN PAPERBACK: 978-1-80587-655-7

Entrance to Enchanted Realms

In the hall where unicorns prance,
And gnomes throw parties, what a chance!
A squeaky hinge and colorful light,
Bring all the silliness to the night.

A cat in a hat gives a wink,
While fish in tuxedos start to drink.
With laughter bubbling from the floor,
Who knew the world's a joke galore?

The Key of Midnight Fantasies

A key that's shaped like a rubber duck,
Unlocks a world of fanciful luck.
A land where socks dance on their own,
And talking sponges claim the throne.

In this realm of silly surprises,
A cupcake sings and never despises.
With every turn, a giggle spills,
And life is just a thrill of thrills.

Passageway to Wishful Realities

Through a tunnel of spaghetti strands,
You'll find a place where laughter stands.
With marshmallow clouds and jellybean trees,
Where the sun bounces, giggling with ease.

A duck in pajamas struts around,
Telling puns that echo profound.
Each step a chuckle, each step a dance,
In this odd world, you take your chance.

Where Visions Unfold

Beneath the arch of wobbly dreams,
A world where nothing's as it seems.
With pirates riding on candy canes,
And rumors spread by friendly trains.

The dragons here will bake you pies,
With blueberry eyes and winked goodbyes.
Every peek reveals a surprise,
Where joy and laughter dance and rise.

Boundless Horizons Await

Knock, knock, who is there?
A cat with a flair!
It prances and struts,
In shoes far too rare.

Beyond the sill, a wild ride,
With penguins who slide.
They dance on the lawn,
Oh, laughter's our guide.

The neighbor's lawn gnomes join in,
With antics that spin.
They juggle and twirl,
The fun's just begin!

So open wide, come along,
Join the comical throng.
With hats made of cheese,
Together we'll sing our song.

The Whispering Archways

Through arches that giggle,
As echoes do wiggle.
In shadows, squirrels chat,
With antics that jiggle.

The walls bear tales old,
Where laughter is bold.
A bunny whispers secrets,
In stories untold.

As you stroll past the frame,
You'll find laughter's game.
With whoopee cushions round,
There's never a shame!

So slip through this place,
With giggles, you'll race.
In a world where you're free,
To be silly with grace.

The Mysterious Latch

A latch that just giggles,
With tickles and wiggles.
It pops with a laugh,
As silliness jiggles.

What's hiding behind?
A hedgehog maligned,
Who wears a top hat,
And dances combined.

With balloons made of cake,
And pies that won't break,
Adventure awaits,
Make haste for fun's sake.

So lift up the bar,
Where jokes travel far.
Let's tease and delight,
And discover bizarre.

Enchantment's Embrace

In a realm full of mishaps,
Where laughter perhaps,
The sun wears a hat,
And dances with slaps.

Chasing shadows that bounce,
And pillows that flounce.
The mice are all chefs,
Who cook while they pounce.

With winks and with cheers,
We'll conquer our fears.
For every lost shoe,
Brings laughter and tears.

So, step through the haze,
In this whimsical maze.
We'll tickle the night,
And linger in plays.

Step into the Unknown

With socks that don't quite match,
The cat is my only guide,
She leads me down the hall,
While giggling at my stride.

A map I made with crayons,
To places I've never been,
Adventure in the pantry,
Where snacks become a scene.

I tip-toe past the fridge,
A land of yogurt hills,
Daring to brave the heights,
Of cookie crumb-filled thrills.

But then a flash of light,
A sandwich on a plate,
I'm swallowed by the mustard,
And now I'm stuck—oh, fate!

Veil of Tomorrow

Tomorrow holds a promise,
Wrapped in bubble wrap,
But knowing my luck well,
I'll trip on it—a trap.

I peek beneath the curtain,
To see what's lurking there,
A dancing pickle spreads joy,
With flair beyond compare.

A pogo stick adventure,
In pajama bottoms loose,
I bounce right past the clock,
Now time's my biggest moose!

Each tick-tock's a giggle,
In this unpredictable race,
I chase the dreams ahead,
With a yarn ball's gentle grace.

Latch to Luminous Hopes

I found a magic latch,
That glows a brilliant blue,
It opens to a world,
Where silly things come true.

A dragon with a bowtie,
Tells jokes that make me wheeze,
I roll upon the floor,
Laughing till I freeze.

There's candy made of pizza,
And ice cream on a tree,
I swing from gumdrop branches,
In blissful jubilee!

But just when I was soaring,
A cloud of giggles swarmed,
I lapsed into a fit,
Of laughter—I was warmed!

Hinge of Hidden Realities

Behind that creaky hinge,
A world of jumbled cheer,
Where jellybeans do salsa,
And cookies mellow dear.

I step into the chaos,
With sneakers white and new,
But they stick to the floor,
Like marshmallows, who knew?

The toaster starts to chatter,
While waffles tune a band,
They serenade the butter,
As I eat what's at hand!

In this wacky place,
Where laughter lights the night,
I'll dance upon a pancake,
And everything feels right!

Circles of Celestial Visions

In socks of polka dots, I fly,
A spaceship made of mashed up pie.
Through rings of laughter spun so bright,
I chase the moon, then hug it tight.

With cupcakes dancing on the stars,
And dancing bears that drive my car.
A comet swings, I take a seat,
We zoom past worlds where llamas greet.

Jogging through clouds of whipped up cream,
A jellybean becomes my dream.
The universe can tickle too,
While unicorns play peekaboo.

So join me on this cosmic ride,
Where giggles burst and twinklings slide.
On circles bright, I'll spin and sway,
Let joy and fun both lead the way.

Bridge to Beautiful Realities

A bridge of rainbows spans the air,
With jellyfish dancing everywhere.
I hop on frogs with candy hats,
While tumbling through the chattiest chats.

The trolls debate with silly quips,
How fish wear boots and pull some tricks.
With giggles bright, we cross each wave,
To find a land where silliness saves.

Lollipops grow tall like trees,
While ants juggle pies with ease.
A river sings a silly song,
And invites us all to hop along.

On this bridge where laughter flows,
Through every turn, my spirit glows.
Reality bends and twists with glee,
In this place where fun runs free.

Opening of Infinite Horizons

A door to giggles swings so wide,
Where rubber chickens take a ride.
With waffles flying through the sky,
I watch the squirrels play and try.

Horizons stretch with silly sights,
Of dancing toasters reaching heights.
A garden blooms with jokes and puns,
Where every laugh is packed with fun.

I slip on shoes of bubble wrap,
While monkeys play a carnival map.
Infinite sights that tickle my brain,
A world where joy is never plain.

So open wide those endless gates,
With pandemonium that captivates.
Where silliness reigns and nothing's grim,
In this great land where hopes swim.

Doorway to Daring Adventures

There once was a door, quite bizarre,
With knobs shaped like jelly, not far.
A twist and a turn,
To places to learn,
It led to a land with a car!

A garden of socks, all alone,
With talking pillows, and a drone.
They brewed up a stew,
That glowed bright and blue,
And danced with a cat made of bone.

The roads were all paved with sweet treats,
Where gumdrops replaced all the seats.
A hiccup would send,
You flying, my friend,
On adventures of laughs and of feats.

So knock on this door, take the chance,
With giggles and twirls, learn to dance.
For wacky and wild,
Like a curious child,
A daydream can lead to romance!

Touching the Other Side

Behind a small door, a cow flies,
In pajamas with polka dot ties.
He giggles and sings,
Of magical things,
Like pizza that rolls and replies.

The walls made of candy and cheer,
Grow brighter each time you come near.
With marshmallow chairs,
And chocolate flares,
You'll live in a world without fear.

You'll hop on the clouds made of cream,
As dragons serve large cups of dream.
They'll tell you a tale,
Of a fish with a pail,
Who swims in a wild, wobbly stream.

So open the latch with a grin,
For laughter awaits you within.
With good vibes galore,
This space is a score,
And joy is the prize you will win!

Soft Knocks of Serendipity

A riddle resides in this frame,
With whispers of giggles and fame.
Just tap on the wood,
It might do some good,
And grant you a moment of game.

The knob turns to bubbles and squeaks,
With squirrels who wear fancy techniques.
They juggle with ease,
And dance in the breeze,
While knitting odd sweaters for peaks.

With portals to worlds full of fun,
Each corner reveals something done.
A disco ball spins,
With laughter that wins,
And everyone joining as one.

So knock on this place with delight,
Your worries will vanish from sight.
For every small crack,
Opens joy with a whack,
And shines ever bright through the night!

Embrace of the Entrée

Through this quaint entrance of cheer,
You'll find a strange feast, lend an ear.
A llama in hats,
Now brings you some bats,
To serve you a pie made of beer.

The table is covered in pies,
With whipped cream that sings in the skies.
Each bite is a laugh,
On a silly path,
To tickle your taste buds with sighs.

Whetstones and spoons start to dance,
As forks do a fun little prance.
They slice through the air,
With stories to share,
In a feast that will make your heart glance.

So step through this archway with glee,
Where whimsy is served, not just tea.
In flavors so bright,
With each joyful bite,
It's a banquet of pure ecstasy!

Thresholds of Imagination

Knock, knock, who is there?
A cat in a hat with flair.
He juggles fish on a tightrope,
Sipping soda, full of hope.

Unicorns dance on the lawn,
Teaching squirrels to play a song.
The treehouse is a spaceship, don't you see?
With marshmallow clouds floating glee.

A tuba plays in the pickle jar,
While gummy bears strum guitars.
Lollipop rain pours from the sky,
As broccoli flies, oh my, oh my!

The garden gnomes hold a debate,
On whether spiders make good mates.
With laughter echoing loud and free,
Imagination is the key, you see!

Gateway to Whispers

Behind the curtain, secrets hide,
A penguin surfing a playful tide.
Whispers giggle when they're caught,
Like butterflies in a candy pot.

There's a dragon, but don't be scared,
He just wants a friend who's shared.
With jellybeans glued on his scales,
And dreams that ride on wobbly sails.

A dance-off between shadows grows,
With disco lights from giant toes.
The moon winks at the laughter sound,
As silly sillies spin around.

Cupcakes rainbows can't resist,
The frosted treats you can't persist.
As whispers turn to boisterous yells,
In this world of quirky spells!

Portals of Possibility

A door swings wide, a rainbow spills,
With penguins wearing tiny frills.
Jump through puddles made of cheer,
Where chocolate rivers flow right here.

The walls are painted polka dots,
While bunnies play with coffee pots.
They brew a latte with whipped cream,
And launch it high, a frothy dream.

A trampoline of marshmallow fluff,
Where laughter flies, a world of stuff.
Catch the giggles, wrap them tight,
As creatures dance under starlit light.

On the other side, pie fights commence,
With giggling gnomes, a joyful suspense.
In this place, reality bends,
And every silly journey transcends.

Beyond the Veil of Slumber

When bedtime calls, the mischief wakes,
A circus formed of silly snakes.
They juggle nightlights, toss and spin,
While teddy bears laugh, the fun begins.

A sleepy moon with twinkling eyes,
Conducts the stars in funny ties.
With a giggle, the wise old owl
Paints stories where strange critters prowl.

Pillow forts rise like castles grand,
Guarded by ducks, a quacking band.
The night unveils its playful tease,
With dreams that dance like leaves in breeze.

So close your eyes, embrace the fun,
In slumber's lands where joy is spun.
With every snooze, a laugh unfurls,
In this realm of whimsical pearls.

Channel of Creative Journeys

A canvas splashed with paint and cheer,
I tripped on thoughts, oh dear, oh dear!
My muse ran off, a silly sprite,
In bunny slippers, out of sight.

With crayons drawn from ancient lore,
I scribble storms and gently soar.
A rubber duck, my thinking cap,
On paper ships, I take a nap.

Ideas dance like socks on floors,
With laughter echoing through the doors.
A playful grin, a wink, a jig,
Creativity, it's quite the gig.

So here I float on whimsy's waves,
In lands of giggles, I'm a knave.
With every stroke, the colors clash,
A funny mess, what a splash!

Nook of Enigma

In a corner with a chair so bright,
I ponder puzzles, day and night.
With rubber bands and old knickknacks,
I craft my thoughts and silly acts.

An ancient book that smells like cheese,
Whispers secrets with sass and tease.
A cat that wears a tiny hat,
Snoozes while I try to chat.

With riddles that tumble like a ball,
I trip on laughter, then I fall.
The walls chime in with giggles loud,
A nook of fun, it draws a crowd.

So here in this whims' delight,
I craft my dreams by day and night.
Each twist and turn, a jolly spree,
A riddle shared with you and me!

Rift of Reality

Through a crack in the scope of day,
I peek where silliness holds sway.
A chicken dances in a tie,
While donuts fly like birds on high.

The world is twisted, upside-down,
With giggles sprouting from the ground.
I juggle socks and sneeze out pies,
Reality shimmies, oh what a surprise!

A toaster sings a jukebox tune,
As stars play hopscotch 'neath the moon.
With cotton candy clouds so bright,
I ride the breeze with pure delight.

In this rift where laughs abound,
Joy is the language all around.
So come and join this silly spree,
In a dream where fun is key!

Intersection of Longing

At the corner where wishes collide,
I dream of cupcakes, far and wide.
With sprinkles raining from the sky,
I leap for joy, oh me, oh my!

My heart thumps loud like thunderclaps,
As I chase rainbows and silly hats.
The universe winks and gives me a shove,
Guiding me through this maze of love.

In every giggle, hope does bloom,
While bubbles burst in a sneeze-filled room.
With marshmallow clouds that float above,
This intersection dances with love.

So here I stand with dreams to share,
In playful whims, we light the air.
At this crossroads, laughter's the theme,
So join my merry, silly dream!

Arch of Untold Stories

Underneath the archway wide,
Socks and sandals tucked inside,
A cat with shades sips lemonade,
While ducks in bow ties dance parades.

A wall of frames with hats askew,
Each tells a tale, each one is new,
A snail on skates goes whizzing by,
With jellybeans that giggle high.

The paint is peeling, colors clash,
A skateboard flies with raucous splash,
In this wild realm where jesters reign,
I scratch my head, but it's insane.

Laughter echoes, strokes of glee,
Where dreams are spun on whimsy's spree,
A tapestry of quirks unbound,
In this archway, joy is found.

Key to the Heart's Yearning

Beneath the mat, the key does hide,
Next to a frog who's full of pride,
He croaks a tune in quirky rhyme,
While ants throw parties, all in time.

A door that's painted bright and bold,
With stories of mischief never told,
A squirrel with shades holds court up high,
As pizza slices float on by.

Unlocking laughter with each twist,
A genie laughs, but does not insist,
He brews up dreams in a frying pan,
While fruit flies dance in a merry band.

With every creak, discoveries bloom,
Hot air balloons fill up the room,
Here in this realm of jester's jest,
My heart's adventure truly rests.

Borderland of Beliefs

In a land where pigeons wear hats,
And talk of politics with cats,
The trees gossip in whispers low,
As clouds play tag in a vibrant show.

A bridge made of marshmallows springs,
Where frogs and mice discuss their things,
Each step a bounce, each laugh a leap,
In this borderland, secrets keep.

In this space where oddities meet,
The grass complains of silly feet,
As dreams take shape in a wacky form,
Juggling stories, a hilarious norm.

Join the parade on the edge of glee,
With mermaids sipping iced tea,
This borderland of belief can prove,
That laughter is the best dance move.

Portal of Inner Landscapes

A portal swirls with purple light,
Where nothings argue, and wrongs feel right,
A goldfish raps, a thrill to hear,
While clouds debate who's the best chef here.

In landscapes drawn with crayons bright,
The sun wears shades, the moon is light,
A trampoline springs to moonlit dreams,
Where chocolate rivers flow with screams.

Giraffes in tuxedos strut the scene,
Complaining of everyone being mean,
Pizza slices fly without a care,
In this funny realm we freely share.

So through the portal, we leap and bound,
Where giggles echo and joy is found,
In inner landscapes, wild and free,
Where every moment is a comedy.

Threshold of Enigma

At the edge of my porch, a cat starts to dance,
Twirling and leaping, in a fanciful trance.
It knocks on my door, with a paw full of glee,
I can't help but laugh; what a sight to see!

A hat made of cheese, it's wearing with pride,
A curious nugget, my brain tries to hide.
Whispers of secrets float in the air,
I finally decide, it's time for a dare!

Picking up socks that have gone on a spree,
I venture outside with a splash of esprit.
The doorknob is sticky, does it want to chat?
Turning it gently, I'm met by a bat!

With cookies and laughter, they all gather near,
The squirrels are feasting, it's my party here.
As shadows begin dancing under the moon,
I wonder if craziness is coming too soon!

Gatekeeper of Serendipity

Knock, knock on whimsy, my door shakes with fun,
What's waiting outside when the day's finally done?
A frog on a skateboard, he's racing the breeze,
He shouts, "Join my journey, it's sure to please!"

With donuts and sprinkles, we'll cruise through the town,
Swapping out worries, for laughter and frown.
A goat in a tuxedo gives high-fives to the stars,
Who knew that adventure had wheels and guitars?

A hula hoop wiggle sends shadows in flight,
While rabbits play poker and dance through the night.
The gatekeeper giggles; I ask for a sign,
Turns out it's a pizza with toppings divine!

As I leap into dreams where the funny reigns,
I ponder if sanity ever remains.
With knock-knock jokes floating through laughter's embrace,
I step out and grin, my heart at a pace!

Frontline of Inspiration

In the hallway of wishes, a broom starts to sing,
It sweeps up the thoughts that the day might bring.
The walls tell stories in colors so bright,
While socks play a duet in the glow of twilight!

A cactus in sunglasses starts sharing its vibe,
As unicorns prance in a fabulous tribe.
My slippers take flight, on a journey so grand,
To a land made of jelly, with jellybean sand!

Transformations abound as I grab for the stars,
The doorknob is winking, oh, look! It's on Mars!
With laughter erupting under rainbow skies,
I can't help but marvel at these wondrous spies.

As curtains of whimsy draw back with a smile,
I invite in the silliness, stay for a while.
In this frontline of joy, absurdity gleams,
With a wink and a nudge, it's the land of dreams!

Passage to Extraordinary

Behind every portal, a giggle awaits,
With a sprinkle of nonsense that barely abates.
A penguin in pajamas takes charge of the show,
He's sliding on rainbows, with nowhere to go!

An octopus chef flips flapjacks with flair,
He juggles pancakes, with syrup to spare.
A trampoline bounces thoughts up to the sky,
Where llamas play chess, with a wink in their eye.

As I step through the doorway, my senses ignite,
Each twist of the knob brings a new delight.
A marshmallow trampoline springs to its height,
While kittens on hoverboards soar out of sight!

With laughter spilling out as the day starts to end,
The passage to oddities never must bend.
So, come join the madness, let silliness reign,
With giggles and grins, oh, what a campaign!

Portico of Potentials

In the hall of wishing well,
Skip through ideas, ring a bell.
Hats of whimsy, shoes of fun,
What's behind? Let's laugh and run.

Socks with polka dots abound,
Tickle your toes, jump around.
Giggles echo, tales unfold,
Pick a dream, let courage bold!

Kites of colors, soaring high,
Pies of laughter baked to pie.
Twirl like a top, dance like a clown,
In this space, we'll never frown!

In quirky shoes, we shall roam,
What a silly place to call home!
With giggly creatures, we explore,
Together, we will laugh and roar!

Corridor of the Imaginative

Dragons ride on rainbow beams,
Sipping ice cream, living dreams.
Running past the paint-splashed walls,
Echoes of laughter bounce and calls.

Mirrors that giggle when you smile,
Trampolines bounce, let's stay awhile!
With socks that match the brightest star,
We'll jump and soar, not go too far.

Chasing shadows, making friends,
Where silly nonsense never ends.
Dance with chairs; let's not be shy,
In this corridor, we'll learn to fly!

Through halls of color, joy ignites,
Every corner holds new delights.
Unlock your heart, it's time to play,
In this wacky world, we'll sway!

Entry to Fantastical Realms

Open wide a curtain bright,
Where gnomes sing songs that take flight.
A sliding slide made just for fun,
Racing on beams, we all can run.

Carpets that tickle your soles,
Here, silly mischief unrolls.
Join the parade of singing shoes,
In this realm, there's never to lose!

Cupcakes dance with sprinkles, bright,
Frogs in tuxedos, what a sight!
Jump on clouds like fluffy puff,
With laughter here, we'll have enough!

With magic hats upon our heads,
We'll tumble, giggle, and play instead.
In fantastical realms, dreams gleam,
It's time to laugh, and let's all dream!

Latch of Infinite Paths

A latch clicks with a friendly sound,
Unlocking joy that knows no bound.
Wacky pathways twist and turn,
Where every corner, new friends yearn.

With peppermint trees that dance and sway,
In this place, we'll laugh and play!
Chocolate rivers, sweet and wide,
Grab your float; let's take a ride!

Through tunnels of giggles, we glide,
In upside-down worlds, we'll reside.
Juggling thoughts like rubber balls,
Let's tumble and pop, break down the walls!

A latch ajar with mental keys,
In laughter's breeze, we're sure to please.
Adventure calls, so let's embark,
To find our way and leave a mark!

Doorways to the Unseen

In a hall of whispers, I found a hook,
With a sign that read, "No peeking, just look!"
I opened it wide, to my surprise,
Came a parade of squirrels in tuxedo ties.

They danced on the ceiling, flipped over my shoes,
Fetching balloons, while singing the blues.
One squirrel took a bow, then slipped on a pie,
Who knew blunders could make laughter fly high?

A door of laughter, what a quirky sight,
Where shadows giggle and tickle the night.
With each rattle and rumble, the walls took a stand,
And out popped a band, playing jazz with a hand.

So knock on my door, if you're feeling low,
Let in the jesters, let their laughter grow.
For hidden in corners, waiting for glee,
Are dreams made of riddles, just waiting for me!

The Arch of Hopeful Slumber

Through the archway of pillows, I drift with a sigh,
Where fairies in pajamas giggle and fly.
They throw sparkly dreams, like confetti at play,
"Oh dear, the cat's napping! Please, let her stay!"

One fairy overslept, got tangled in yarn,
As her slippers got stuck on a soft, plushy barn.
They opened a portal to laughers and beams,
Trading my worries for delicious weird dreams.

In this place of delight, the moon wears a hat,
While singing sweet songs with the twinkling chat.
I bounced on the clouds, my slippers were light,
Dancing with giggles 'til morning's first light.

So creep in your jammies, bring all your cheer,
The dreams are a party! So no need to fear.
With each little giggle in the archway's embrace,
You'll find a sweet slumber in a magical space!

Inviting Shadows of Tomorrow

Beneath a bright blanket, shadows convene,
They plot silly schemes, quite absurd and obscene.
One shadow's a dancer, the other a clown,
Juggling odd items they scrounged from the town.

With a head of a cabbage, and feet made of cheese,
They twist and they tumble with whimsical ease.
Tomorrow is coming, but today is the show,
With laughter and mayhem, they steal the whole glow.

A shadow in pink grabbed a hat off the shelf,
Declared, "I'm the king!" but forgot about stealth.
They tumbled and fumbled, all giggles and glee,
As I watched from the couch, feeling quite carefree.

So if you hear chuckles when the sun's drifting low,
Invite those odd shadows, let the laughter flow.
For tomorrow may whisper of dreams yet unseen,
But tonight is for jesters and moments between!

Openings to Celestial Journeys

An awning of stardust, an entrance to play,
Where ticklish comets sing through the Milky Way.
A spaceship of marshmallows floats snug at the door,
With candy canes waving, "Come, explore some more!"

They giggle and grace, in a chorus so bright,
As I strap in my boots and launch into the night.
Around me the planets start spinning with joy,
A galactic parade, oh, what a ploy!

One comet wore glasses, a smirk on its face,
While sharing old tales of a faraway place.
"Don't eat too much stardust, it's hard on the heart,
But please, feel free to sample, it's a cosmic art!"

So if you hear laughter when gazing at stars,
Just imagine the journeys that whisk us from Mars.
With openings ready, adventure takes flight,
In a universe humming with glee and delight!

Opening to the Unseen

A tiny key, a twist of fate,
What lies beyond? Oh, I can't wait!
A cat in boots, a dancing bear,
Mismatched socks float in the air.

Each knock invites a giggle spree,
A talking plant says, "Come and see!"
A rainbow slides down from the roof,
With jellybeans as solid proof.

The fridge hums tunes that make me sway,
While spoons and forks begin to play.
A circus mouse on roller skates,
In foggy air, he makes his mates.

With silly hats and giant shoes,
This quirky world has lots to choose.
Adventures bloom and never cease,
As curious hearts find sheer release.

Passage to Reverie

Through this arch, we leap and bound,
Where ice cream clouds drift all around.
A pogo stick that flies so high,
And talking pancakes fill the sky.

A carousel spins with a funny twist,
Pigs in goggles—who could resist?
Cotton candy trees, oh delight,
With laughter sparkling through the night.

Each echo tickles like a breeze,
As rainbows drip from frothy seas.
With silly sailors on a quest,
Adventure waits, it's for the best!

In wacky realms where giggles live,
Embrace the joy that dreams can give.
So leap on in, don't miss the fun,
This endless ride has just begun!

Welcome Mat of Wonders

A welcome mat that giggles loud,
It rolls itself beneath the crowd.
With doors that swing on rubber hinges,
And walls that hum sweet, silly jinges.

A leaping frog in a tutu bright,
Chasing shadows that dance in light.
A slide made of chocolate, oh so sweet,
Inviting everyone to take a seat.

With giant mushrooms all around,
And toadstools playing hopscotch sound.
A bird that croons the silliest tune,
While crickets dressed in suits debate at noon.

Each creak and squeak brings forth delight,
As giggles spread beyond the night.
In this wonderland, we play,
Forever young, come join the fray!

Frame of Infinite Visions

Through this frame, the silliness grows,
A dancing ghost in polka clothes.
With socks that giggle on the floor,
And whispers feasting on folklore.

A dizzy cat with a jester's hat,
Makes friends with a wise, old, strange brat.
A clock that jokes with every tick,
As beans on toast begin to kick.

Painting dreams on the wallpaper,
With twisty vines that start to drape.
Where every glance leads to some cheer,
And funny faces draw near.

So come and peek inside the frame,
Where every heart can play the game.
Unravel worlds both bright and bold,
In this silly place, let joy unfold!

Steps into the Realm of Reverie

A wobbly path lies ahead,
With squeaky shoes and a rubber fed.
Each toe wiggles in curious glee,
To a place where cats climb trees.

In dreamland, ice cream rains from the sky,
And zebras wear ties, oh my, oh my!
Jumping on clouds, we bounce and glide,
While dancing squirrels take us for a ride.

The sun wears sunglasses, a wise old chap,
Giggling as turtles take a nap.
With jellybeans growing on vine-draped trees,
We feast while tickling wild, naughty bees.

So take off your shoes, enjoy the flight,
Embrace the silly, it's pure delight!
In this land of whimsy, laughter rolls,
As we leap through hoops made of jelly rolls.

The Threshold of Starry Nights

At the edge of the moon, I trip and fall,
Where coffee cups hold secrets tall.
Starfish in tuxedos run the show,
Singing tunes only owls seem to know.

With jigsaw puzzles in clouded air,
Find the pieces, if you dare.
Rockets made of candy soar high,
While marshmallow giraffes peek from the sky.

A bicycle rides on the Milky Way,
With gummy bears leading the way.
We flip-flop through constellations bright,
Laughing 'til dawn settles the night.

So let your dreams be a silly parade,
Where rubber ducks waltz unafraid.
In the glow of stars, let worries flee,
And join the dance with glee in spree.

Latch to the Land of What-Ifs

The latch clicks open; oh what a sight!
Penguins in pajamas, ready to fight!
In this land of might-bes, bats play chess,
While turtles bust moves in a crazy dress.

What if the sun could cook a pie?
And clouds turned to marshmallows floating by?
Unicorns munch on crispy gold flakes,
As fish in sombreros dance with snakes.

There's a rainbow slide made of jellybeans,
Where candy canes grow like little machines.
We twirl with the breeze, as we chase a kite,
That hums the tune of a chicken's delight.

So latch on tightly, let reality bend,
Forget the clock, let imagination extend.
In this whimsical world, all doubts round,
With laugh-echoes swirling, magic is found.

Glimmers Beyond Boundaries

Funky stars sparkle in a dance-off,
Flipping and spinning, they twirl and scoff.
On a trampoline made of bright blue cheese,
We bounce with jellyfish, float with ease.

A raccoon in shades fits snugly a chair,
While questioning every piece of air.
Bubblegum clouds with smiles so wide,
Invite our friends for a glitter ride.

What's behind that crooked old tree?
A sock convention just for you and me!
Where each one wears its own fashion flair,
And disco balls shine in the fresh air.

So take a few steps into the unknown,
Where laughter and whimsy are brightly sown.
In the glimmers of fun, let hearts expand,
And do a pratfall—ain't life just grand?

Passage to the Fabled

In a land where socks can walk,
And dancing cats all like to talk.
A rubber chicken flew on by,
Wearing a hat, oh me, oh my!

Rainbows rain and gumdrops fall,
With candy trees that grow so tall.
A fish in boots learned how to skate,
Inviting friends, oh this is great!

Jumping squirrels in suits so bright,
Stealing tarts in broad daylight.
The moon wears glasses, quite absurd,
And quacks like ducks, oh have you heard?

Throw a party with a twist,
Invite the gnomes, you can't resist!
In this land of topsy-turvy,
Every moment's fun and wordy!

Breath of New Beginnings

A toaster dreams of buttered toast,
While dishwashers brag, they love to boast.
The oven sings a happy tune,
As kitchen gadgets dance a swoon.

The mop does ballet, spins around,
While dust bunnies gather, unbound.
With every flip and silly twist,
They celebrate, oh how they tryst!

The fridge throws parties, bright and loud,
With leftovers dancing proud and bowed.
Salads waltz and cakes do cheer,
While oranges juggle, never fear!

In this kitchen, joy takes flight,
With laughter echoing every night.
When pots and pans create a show,
You'll feel the magic start to flow!

Realm of the Fantastical

Once upon a pickle jar,
Lived a silly dancing star.
It twirled and swayed with all its might,
While a bear in pajamas joined the fight.

A waffle bike zoomed through the air,
With syrup flies that didn't care.
Together they raced spots and stripes,
Creating wild and funny gripes.

Monkeys in top hats, sipping tea,
Chasing rainbows with glee, oh me!
They played hopscotch on the clouds,
While elephants cheered, drawing crowds.

Suddenly a cupcake flew by,
With glitter sprinkles reaching high.
In this place where laughter rules,
Every moment's filled with silly tools!

Portal to Whimsicality

In a yard of silly shoes,
A grasshopper sings the morning blues.
Caterpillars play with strings,
While frogs discuss the weather and things.

A pond made of jelly, wobbly with cheer,
Holds tap-dancing turtles, oh dear, oh dear!
They slip and slide, what a hilarious sight,
Under the umbrella of a bright, twinkling light.

A giant donut rolls on by,
Sending sprinkles up to the sky.
While giggling ants prepare a feast,
With chocolate syrup, to say the least!

In this land of light and shade,
Silly tales are made and played.
So step inside, if you're brave,
Where nonsense reigns and laughs we crave!

Frame of Boundless Horizons

In the frame, a cat looks out,
Plotting dreams, without a doubt.
A run to chase a silly bird,
Yet what he catches? Not a word.

The mailbox talks, or so they say,
It tells the mailman to delay.
With letters flying in the breeze,
The postman giggles, if you please!

A hat that flies upon the breeze,
It wanders off, oh what a tease!
Chasing thoughts, it twirls around,
In this mad world, fun is found!

The fence can dance, it shakes with glee,
While weeds do cluck, just wait and see!
A party here, an ale there too,
In this garden, wild and blue!

Pathway to Secret Gardens

A squirrel walks and wears a tie,
He tells a joke that makes me cry!
The flowers giggle, bloom in jest,
This pathway leads to nature's fest.

A sign that points to nowhere good,
Where all the plants now act like food.
The carrots dance, the peas flip hats,
While bunnies huff, "We're not like cats!"

A pathway full of hidden traps,
For sleepy bees and napping chaps.
Each step I take, I count my luck,
For here, I'll find my picnic pluck!

The pumpkin laughs, a jolly fellow,
It rolls around, quite bright and yellow.
In secret gardens, dreams take flight,
With cotton candy clouds in sight!

Passageway of Dreams

A hall of socks, mismatched and bold,
Whispers secrets, or so I'm told.
The shadows dance with giggly shoes,
They play hide and seek, you can't refuse!

Inside this passage, there's a chime,
That only rings at silly times.
It sings of cake and sprinkles fair,
While jellybeans float in the air!

A slide of slides that leads to fun,
Where every step's a wobbly run.
And giggles echo off the walls,
In this weird place where laughter calls!

So take a step, don't miss the chance,
For here, the dreams just love to dance.
The passage wide opens my heart,
In every laugh, I find my start!

Lullaby of the Threshold

At the threshold, a rooster sings,
He flaps his wings, and somewhat stings.
A lullaby with notes so bright,
It sets the cat to dance at night!

With waltzing mice and cheese on tape,
A grand ballet, the strangest shape.
They pirouette on crumbs so fine,
While shadows giggle, join the line!

A doorknob that spins with glee,
Luring you in for tea, oh me!
It brews a potion just for fun,
And every sip brings out a pun!

In every creak, a rhyme so sweet,
The laughter lingers at your feet.
A lullaby to catch your dream,
Where silliness reigns, as we all beam!

Pathways to the Heart's Desire

Knock, knock, is anybody home?
The cat's in charge, chasing foam.
A sandwich waits, just out of reach,
While squirrels plot as they silently screech.

Balloons in colors, floating bright,
Join my quest for cake tonight.
The map is marked with scribbles and glee,
A treasure hunt just for me!

The sun pops up and starts to sway,
Finding socks that run away.
There's magic here, or so they claim,
But where's that pesky sock with the little name?

A cup of tea on a bouncy chair,
Turns into a ride with a furry bear.
With laughter loud and mischief grand,
We'll jump to worlds, hand in hand.

Echoes at the Edge of Tales.

Once upon a time, a dragon cooked,
Pasta made from a spellbook.
With marinara that glowed like gold,
It danced right off its plate, not bold.

A fairy sneezed, and the stars fell down,
Landing softly on a sleepy town.
The giggles spread, like butter on toast,
As all the villagers gathered close.

Magic puddles served with giggles,
Made everyone bounce and do the wiggles.
But beware the gnome who loves to tease,
He'll swap your hat for a swarm of bees!

At the edge of dreams and silly schemes,
Stories dance like sunlight beams.
Join the laughter, don't you pout,
For fun is what it's all about!

Thresholds of Imagination

In a land where shoes can walk alone,
And millions of books call you their own.
The ceiling fans spin tales of cheer,
As kittens practice flying near.

A turkey wears a party hat,
While shadows spin like a jazzy cat.
With marshmallow clouds that bounce on high,
It's easy to laugh and just comply.

Rainbows sprout from the garden gate,
As laughter bubbles, never late.
Planting dreams like candy seeds,
Tending joy, for all our needs.

Bouncing boats on jelly seas,
Imagining flavors of candy trees.
With every leap and happy shout,
Our world of dreams is what it's about!

Gateway to Whispers

A door creaks open, whispers swirl,
Shimmery shouts from a giggling girl.
Fluffy clouds invite a hop,
Where even the grumpy cannot stop!

Socks converse in a playful spree,
Arguing over who stole the tea!
With rubber ducks leading the parade,
Every shadow dances, unafraid.

A monster with googly eyes,
Swaps stories under cotton skies.
With tickles shared and tales that glide,
The laughter echoes deep inside.

Slide down rainbows, spin with glee,
Let every dream be a cup of tea.
In the land where wonders reside,
We'll hop and laugh with hearts open wide!

Meta of Marvels

In pajamas I glide, with my cape on tight,
A battle with dust bunnies, oh what a sight!
The toaster rebels, sparks flying in jest,
Breakfast defeats me, and I must confess.

A spider's web dance, all too grand,
It wins the award for the messiest strand.
I trip on my shoes, still untied,
In this circus of chaos, I take great pride.

The cat's my sidekick, plotting his scams,
He takes all the treats, while I'm busy with jams.
Together we scheme, with giggles galore,
In this wild adventure, who could ask for more?

With a twist and a turn, we launch into glee,
Who knew the broomstick could also fly free?
Embracing the madness, I leap with a cheer,
In our house of wonder, there's nothing to fear.

Peep Hole to Possibilities

A tiny peephole, oh what a view,
I see gnomes in the garden, all covered in dew.
They sip on their tea, with hats tall and proud,
Laughing at squirrels, oh they're quite loud!

A raccoon makes pancakes, flipping with flair,
While a hedgehog joins in, to show that he's there.
They dance on the lawn, a delightful parade,
And I can't help but grin at the fun they have made.

With a wink and a chuckle, I join their grand quest,
To put on a show, in my pajamas, no less!
We twirl through the garden, kicking up leaves,
In a symphony of laughter, oh how our hearts tease.

Peeking through moments, I see all the fun,
Life's a grand circus, and we're not yet done!
In this magical realm, where whimsy is king,
I'll forever keep watching, oh what joy they bring!

Opening for the Soul's Flight

An umbrella's not just for keeping dry,
Oh no, it's a rocket for dreams that can fly!
With a flick and a twist, I'm off to the moon,
Sipping stardust smoothies, I'll be back really soon.

The couch is a cloud, with cushions ablaze,
Inviting me in for some whimsical days.
It's a palace of giggles, where laughter runs free,
With all of my stuffed friends, just waiting for tea!

We'll build forts from blankets, with towers of fun,
The dragon will guard us, his job's never done.
As we ride on our laughter, through giggles that bloom,
In this realm of nonsense, there's always more room.

In a world full of wonders that sparkle and shine,
There's adventure awaiting, just grab a kerfuffle line!
So open the gateway, let your spirit sprout,
For through these delights, is what life's all about.

Invitation to the Imagined

Come step through the curtain, it's a wild retreat,
Where broccoli dances, and carrots have feet.
The toaster is singing, while the kettle sways,
In this party of flavors, we're lost in a craze.

The fridge is a portal to lands of delight,
Where pickles are pirates, sailing through night.
They're mapping out treasures beneath all the snacks,
With donuts for ships, oh watch out for attacks!

A marshmallow army stands ready to fight,
Against the onslaught of jellybeans' might.
They're stocking the pantry, laying their claim,
In this glorious tempest, we all share the fame.

So grab your imagination, it's time to play,
In this land of the silly, where nonsense can sway.
With laughter as our compass, let joy be our guide,
In this invitation to whimsy, let's all take a ride!

The Canopy of Silent Aspirations

Beneath a sky of bubblegum,
I found a chair that felt so numb.
It giggled back with marshmallow sighs,
As cotton candy clouds danced in the skies.

A squirrel wore spectacles, reading a book,
As I tried to blend in, with a baffled look.
With dreams that sprouted like mushrooms in spring,
A jazz band of frogs began to sing.

The grass talked gossip, a real chitchat,
About a lazy puppy and a top-hat cat.
I asked for wisdom, they offered me pie,
"Take a slice, and give the world a try!"

So I slipped on shoes of banana peel,
And pranced in circles, oh what a deal!
In this canopy where laughter grows,
Every aspiration wears silly clothes.

Steps into the Canvas of Cosmos

I stepped on stars with polka-dot feet,
Each step a whisper, so light and sweet.
The moon handed me a paintbrush of dreams,
To color the night with custard creams.

Comets became comical roller coasters,
With twinkling lights and shimmering posters.
I rode with laughter, going splash and clatter,
While alien ducks quacked in cosmic chatter.

Galaxies giggled, a shimmering sight,
While galaxies waltzed with sheer delight.
I painted the universe in stripes and spots,
As meteors steered to connect all the dots.

With each brush stroke, joy seemed to soar,
And painted suns danced on the floor.
In this canvas where whimsy reigned,
Every heartbeat felt uncontained.

Windows to Daydreams

Behind a glass that sparkled bright,
Lies a world of colors, all pure delight.
Jellybeans floated, a sweet, sticky breeze,
While gummy bears danced with such effortless ease.

I peered a bit closer, with curiosity wild,
Saw a unicorn sipping on cocoa, like a child.
With every sip, giggles filled the air,
Balloons of laughter bobbing everywhere.

A cat in pajamas played hopscotch with me,
As taffy rivers flowed sweetly, carefree.
The sun wore sunglasses, lounging in the sky,
And whispered secrets with a wink of an eye.

I opened the window and flew like a kite,
In a swirl of jellyfish and firefly light.
In this realm of whims, I played tag with dreams,
Where joy bubbles over in infinite streams.

Veils of Enchanted Whimsy

In a garden where wishes twirled like dervishes,
I found a frog who played sweet, silly symphonies.
With flowers wearing hats and shoes too bright,
This place was a parade, a pure delight.

Butterflies swapped stories, gossip on a leaf,
While mushrooms giggled, beyond belief.
A snail wore a cape, an adventurer grand,
As daisies sang songs, hand in hand.

I tried to savor each magical bite,
Of dreams served on plates under starlit night.
With cupcakes that giggled and pastries that cheered,
Every moment a treasure, fully endeared.

So I danced with the shadows, in spirals of glee,
In this enchanted veil, I truly felt free.
Where whimsy and laughter conspired in bloom,
Turning every corner into a sunlit room.

Portal of Poetic Possibilities

In a land where socks unite,
And last night's pizza takes flight,
A door made of rhymes ajar,
Singers hum in a candy car.

With jellybeans on petals dance,
Each step a chance, a wobbly prance,
Here unicorns trade jokes galore,
While pineapples gossip on the floor.

A wizard sneezes glitter dust,
And cupcakes giggle, surely they must,
Time spins in a silly loop,
Where marshmallow bears lead a troop.

Tap your feet on the rainbow way,
Join the parade, it's a silly sway,
Hold your hat, be merry and bold,
For possibilities here are never old.

Threshold of Timeless Wonders

Step lightly through this wobbly door,
With a giggle and a dance to explore,
Where clocks spin backward, tick-tock is lost,
And every breath is a laugh at a cost.

Old teacups hold secrets well,
As rubber ducks wish to dwell,
Here lies a map made of jelly,
Leading to a giant sunflower's belly.

Those shadows twist and perform a jig,
While a snail recites riddles quite big,
In forests of candy cane trees,
All join in chorus, it's pure, silly cheese!

Ride the breeze on a purring cat,
Spinning yarns of an elephant fat,
Ceilings painted in bubblegum hues,
Every step down the hall, there's more to amuse.

Gateway to Starlit Aspirations

Open the gate made of twinkling dreams,
Where laughter erupts in glittering streams,
Couch cushions float; in flight, they soar,
While wishes squeal, begging for more.

Stars wear pajamas, winking with grace,
A parade of cats in a race,
Ice cream clouds sprinkle joy below,
In the chandelier of the moon's soft glow.

Leprechauns juggle with pots of gold,
Tickled by tales that never get old,
Hopscotch on comets, we leap with glee,
Synchronized dreams, a wacky jamboree!

So jump through the gate, don't lag behind,
Where every star is wonderfully blind,
On breezy swings, hearts take flight,
In this realm of humor, pure delight.

Entrance to Ephemeral Moments

Welcome to a place where time does flip,
Hiccups of laughter, a silly trip,
Where jellyfish wear tiny top hats,
And the goldfish chatter like cheeky brats.

Clouds do yoga, twist in the air,
While bubbles recite poetry in pair,
Each tickle bursts into a tune,
As tumbleweeds strut and dance in June.

Noses honk like trombones blown,
As cookie monsters claim a throne,
Stairs made of licorice lead you high,
To slide down rainbows, oh my, oh my!

So wander through this frothy gate,
With giggles galore, it's never too late,
Among quirky sights that never cease,
In moments of fun, we find our peace.

The Crossroad of Yearning Paths

Two paths diverged in a silly way,
One led to work, the other to play.
I chose the route with a rubber duck,
But ended up stuck in a pot of muck.

A signpost waved with a grin so wide,
'Pick a direction, take a ride!'
I said, 'I'll go where the giggles flow!'
And stumbled straight into a wiggly show.

A jester appeared with a hat so tall,
He tripped on his feet, then tumbled like a ball.
'Join me dear friend,' he called with glee,
As I laughed and rolled in pure jubilee.

So here I am, at this crossroads odd,
Where choices shine like a yellow facade.
With every misstep, my heart takes flight,
In this wacky maze, every turn feels right.

Framing the Fantastic Fables

With a frame of clouds and a backdrop of cheese,
I painted a tale that could only tease.
A dragon in slippers danced on my wall,
While unicorns jogged—yes, they ran a mall!

The book of tales had a mind of its own,
It whispered sweet nothings—how far I've grown.
A frog in a tux played a lute made of sticks,
He serenaded the moon with his charming tricks.

Pages flipped wildly, as giggles erupted,
A cat in a hat looked ever so flustered.
Came a knock on the frame, 'Is this story real?'
I shrugged and said, 'What a fun squeal!'

So I hug my odd canvas, paintbrush in hand,
With worlds that spin round like a carnival band.
With frames that stretch far as the eye can glance,
I live in this story—a comical dance.

Portal of Secret Histories

Behind the curtain lies a tale untold,
Of socks that wander and kittens that scold.
A portal beckons, with a wink so sly,
Where pancakes twerk and the muffins fly!

A scholar of mischief peeks through the haze,
Whispers of pudding in syrupy maze.
He scribes on a scroll made of jellybeans,
While the wind chimes sing of spaghetti dreams.

Through this gateway, I spy on the quirks,
Of dreams where fish wear their favorite shirts.
With wisdom gathered from fruitcake debates,
I dance in the moonlight with marshmallow mates.

So if you should stumble upon this delight,
Be ready to giggle, to twirl, and take flight.
For in this old portal, as secrets unwind,
You'll find the hiccup that tickles your mind.

The Sill of Inner Reflections

On the windowsill, my thoughts take a peek,
In pajamas adorned with a squeeze of cheek.
A squirrel offered tea from a tin can top,
And debated if carrots could make new blops!

With mirrors that giggle, they show me my face,
'Are you a jester or just out of place?'
I twirl and I spin, in a wobbly fashion,
While ice cream whispers, 'Do I bring you passion?'

A dance in reflection, a loop-de-loop cheer,
Each glance in the glass is a visit from fear.
But bright colors splash as I laugh in delight,
For silliness bubbles at morning dusk light.

So here by the glass, I dream and I jest,
With giggles and grins, I feel truly blessed.
In this thoughtful corner, I'm wild and I'm free,
For silliness blooms in my heart's jubilee.

Entry to the Cosmic Dance

In a waltz of stars, we twirl and spin,
With mismatched socks and a goofy grin.
The moon's our DJ, playing tunes so odd,
While aliens laugh, and a comet nods.

A gumball chandelier hangs from above,
We step on gumdrops, but it's all in love.
They serve us jelly beans right off a plate,
As we dance through worlds, a cosmic fate.

In the swirl of colors, we chuckle and sway,
As the universe throws confetti our way.
No shoes required for this silly spree,
Just keep on twirling, feel wild and free!

With every spin, new friends we make,
A chicken in sunglasses starts to quake.
Hold onto your hats, it'll go awry,
As joy lifts us up, and we fly high!

Welcome to the World of Wishes

In a land where wishes oddly come true,
A squirrel in a tuxedo just said 'How do you do?'
With cupcakes raining from bright, fluffy skies,
And custard-filled clouds that dance with surprise.

A sign welcomes all with a wink and a cheer,
'Forget all your worries, your dreams are near!'
Mermaids juggle jelly, oh what a sight,
While unicorns boogie, bringing pure delight.

The rivers run chocolate, so rich and so sweet,
Shoals of gumdrops make every step a treat.
With laughter like bubbles, we float in the air,
Every wish granted, in this world without care!

So grab a pink donut, jump into the fun,
The land of wishes has only begun.
Here, smiles are currency, happiness reigns,
Join the ruckus, and let go of the chains!

Doorway of Delights

Step right up to a wacky parade,
Where broccoli plays drums and lemons invade.
A door made of candy, it's sticky and bright,
Opens with laughter, a marvelous sight!

With sunglasses on, we meet furry friends,
Who toss us confetti that never quite ends.
Clouds made of marshmallows float overhead,
As we skip through the doorway, adventure ahead!

A slide made of licorice whips us away,
To a land of delight that invites us to play.
Riding on cupcakes, we leap and we shout,
In the doorway of wonders, we twirl about!

So let's dance with the octopus dressed in style,
In our doorway of delights, we linger awhile.
With each laugh and giggle, we relish our fate,
In a candy-coated world, it's never too late!

Beyond the Veil

Beyond the veil, where silliness grows,
Pigs wear top hats and balance on toes.
A rhyming rabbit offers tea made of cheese,
With dandelion pastries, oh what a tease!

Jellyfish tango with a marching band,
While cookies do yoga on soft, fluffy sand.
The sun winks at us from a bright purple sky,
As we laugh out loud, letting worries fly high.

A trampoline river that bounces our hearts,
In a world where imagination plays all the parts.
With smiles infectious, we twirl and we spin,
Life's a grand circus, let the fun begin!

When horizons are sparkly, and wishful delight,
Join the creatures in dancing till the fall of night.
In this magical realm, where quirks come alive,
Together we flourish, together we thrive!

Portal of Possibilities

A door with a wink and a jolly surprise,
Leads to a world where the weirdos all rise.
Painted in colors that dance and explode,
With a doorknob that giggles—it's never a load.

Through this threshold, a cat wears a hat,
Juggling some fish while it chats with a bat.
Unicorns skate on marshmallow floors,
And each time it opens, a new laugh implores.

On Tuesdays, it's filled with spaghetti rain,
And Wednesdays promise some ice cream to gain.
Yet Fridays are wild, with a frog karaoke,
While dancing on clouds that are bright and smoky.

So step right inside, take a chance on the quirk,
Leave your coat on a cloud, let your weirdness work.
Every moment's a giggle, a game to be played,
In this portal of fun, let your worries fade.

Archway to Enchantment

An archway of ribbons and playful surprise,
Leading to places where nonsense can rise.
Balloons with faces float high in the air,
And mushrooms can dance if you join in their flair.

A squirrel with glasses is reading a book,
While fairies trade secrets in every nook.
The fish all wear boots and do cha-cha real slow,
In a whimsical world where the laughter can grow.

Just follow the sparkles and giggling beams,
Past the fountain of candy and chocolate streams.
With each flit and flutter, the silliness grows,
As the archway invites you to let your heart go.

So swing through this portal with a chuckle or two,
And let whimsy enchant you, it's waiting for you.
In this archway of laughter, there's joy to explore,
With each step that you take, you will ask for more.

Entryway to Fantasies

An entryway sparkles with shimmer and cheer,
Where pancakes wear hats and invite you near.
The floor is all jelly, it wobbles and shakes,
While trees drip with syrup and grinning cupcakes.

A giraffe in a tuxedo starts spinning a tale,
As penguins in bowties join in without fail.
Slippers on rabbits hop across the show,
In this goofy place where the oddities flow.

Clouds made of cotton candy drift on by,
As rainbows shoot arrows up into the sky.
With every odd twist from the doorknob's clink,
You'll find more than you bargained—just wait and think.

So step through the portal, let laughter ignite,
In this entryway wild, full of sheer delight.
With each silly smile that drops from the air,
You'll find that your worries are just not that rare.

Crossroads of Aspirations

At a crossroads where whimsy begins to unfold,
You'll meet a bright parrot with stories retold.
He squawks about wishes that dance on a breeze,
While leprechauns juggle their pots full of keys.

A turtle on roller-skates speeds through with flair,
Sharing dreams about places where dragons can share.
The sidewalk is striped like a giant gold brick,
And every odd step makes you laugh till you're sick.

On Thursday, the moon likes to swing on a line,
And Friday's a party with cake and with wine.
Each direction you take offers laughs on a track,
While mermaids on scooters wink back for the crack.

So wander a minute at this joyful cross,
Embrace every twist, worry just might get lost.
For at this wild junction of hopes and of schemes,
The world opens wide to your silliest dreams.

www.ingramcontent.com/pod-product-compliance
Lightning Source LLC
Chambersburg PA
CBHW062111280426
43661CB00086B/463